THE MEDITATION LIFESTYLE

COLUM HAYWARD

The Meditation Lifestyle

With illustrations by Bodel Rikys and
forewords by Jenny Dent and David Barclay

Polair
Publishing

POLAIR PUBLISHING

P O BOX 34886 · LONDON W8 6YR
www.polairpublishing.co.uk

First published July 2012

© Copyright, Colum Hayward 2012

British Library Cataloguing in Publication Data
A catalogue record for this book is available
from the British Library

ISBN 978-1-905398-26-3

Set in 13 on 16.5pt Monotype Joanna
Printed and bound in the UK by Biddles, part of the
MPG Books Group, Bodmin and King's Lynn

Contents

Foreword by Jenny Dent

ON RETREATS and in my work generally I have long been aware of the need for a book of this kind to help people transform their personal 'meditation journey' into a practice that sustains them constantly, every minute. Colum is an inspirational teacher of meditation – I have learnt much from experiencing his technique – and this book allows many more people to share in his teaching.

Colum is working within the White Eagle Lodge to develop our White Eagle School of Meditation and is now leading our new Wisdom School meditation teacher training programme. His depth of knowledge of different faiths and meditation practices makes this book both far-reaching and thought-

Jenny Dent is Mother of the White Eagle Lodge, an international organization founded in 1936, which teaches a path of spiritual unfoldment through healing, service and meditation.

provoking, yet it carries a personal note that speaks to us all as individuals, helping us to find our individual meditation style.

Meditation is for Busy People

David Barclay

IT IS tempting to assume, if you think you are busy, that you don't have time to meditate. Taking time out for private thought sounds like an escape, or at least an indulgence. Meditation, in other words, is for people with time on their hands. And some of us have work to do.

The assumption that meditation, like lunch, is for wimps may be tempting, but it is wrong. Meditation is for busy people. Indeed, it might have been invented for them.

Being busy is fine as far as it goes. There is a certain satisfaction, after all, in 'getting stuff done'. And, on a good day, busy people can do

David Barclay is a former assistant private secretary to the Prime Minister and vice chairman of Kleinwort Benson, the investment bank. He is currently deputy chairman of the John Lewis Partnership and a member of the board of The British Library.

lots for others as well as themselves.

I count myself pretty busy. What with a career spanning government, the City and the boardroom, what with children, and what with elderly parents, time has always seemed in rather short supply.

I have learnt, though, that there are dangers in being busy. Some of these dangers are personal: anxiety, stress, the sense of being overwhelmed by the enormity of one's own to do list. Others can damage those around us, not just family and friends but work colleagues and those for whom we have responsibility. If our brains are too busy, we are likely to be difficult to live with and we risk making bad decisions.

The answer, for busy people, is not to do less. That would be out of character. The answer is to do something a bit different, not more and more of the same; slightly to reorder priorities and allow the opportunity, preferably each day, to reconnect with one's inner self in a moment of calm, unflustered by the passage of time or the imminent expiry of another deadline.

This may be easier said than done. But busy people actually make small adjustments to their priorities all the time. Indeed, they are good at it.

I started my own process of adjustment by attending a series of classes created by Colum Hayward as an introduction to meditation. Much of the wisdom he shared has found its way into this book.

If you are busy, you have already made a start by opening it. You will find that it offers accessible and practical advice on how to give your brain a break and rediscover contentment in a moment of time. If you are busy it could make you more effective as well as happier.

What more could a busy person want?

Meditation ... is for busy people

Acknowledgments

THIS BOOK is dedicated to my students, all of them. No teacher can learn without the process students offer. Although I had been teaching for many years before, my teaching came of age when I took on classes at the Shepherds Bush Healthy Living Centre at the request of its director, Iain Hodgkinson. Many of my students there knew nothing about meditation at all and it taught me the benefits of a very grounded, slow approach to meditation with few prior assumptions about skills. I learnt that to separate out the skills of the meditator gives him/her a surer foundation to his/her practice. I am delighted that several of those students still come to classes ten years later.

I'm also grateful to my own teachers, who include my mother and aunt and my grandmother, and a whole tradition within the White Eagle Lodge, but – since this is a book about the whole of life, and not a confined practice – my teachers are all those who have taught me, wittingly and unwittingly. That even includes those who seem to have hurt or restricted me, often the most powerful teachers of all!

Jenny Beeken got me onto the basic standing pose in this book, and reminded me how inspired my aunt had been by the teaching of Vanda Scaravelli in her book AWAKENING THE SPINE. I make no claims to be a practitioner of the *asanas* myself, and yet the principle in that book I hope infuses this one – if it's for me to say. I'm grateful to Jenny for letting me quote her.

Quotations from White Eagle are all © Copyright, the White Eagle Publishing Trust, and I thank the Trust for permission to use them. Finally, I'm grateful to all who have read the manuscript, and given me useful comments, including Bodel Rikys, Jenny Beeken, Anna Hayward, David Barclay and Mary Goodchild. Lastly, a special tribute of thanks to Romayne Drury, at whose beautiful Tuscan farm I made the breakthrough that finally got the book written.

Introduction

After you are born, a process begins so that soon you are standing on your own two feet. It is perhaps the greatest symbol of independent existence you or I ever have.

Although at that age you are not ready to conceive what is going on intellectually, to stand on two feet requires trust. The most basic trust is that the earth is beneath you to hold you up – something you almost never, even in adult life, will think about (at least until you read this book). Then there is the trust that the muscles you have been developing since birth will support you, and that your innate sense of balance will teach you which ones to use. Lastly in this picture there is also, probably, a trust that a kind mother or father will pick you up when you fall, and that after they have comforted you, you will try again until you feel safe doing it – until trust, balance, muscle strength and the good earth are forgotten and you both stand and walk without thinking about what you are doing. Lesson learned – and forgotten until either you have an accident, or take up meditation!

Right through adult life, then, to stand is the symbol of humanhood: not on four legs like many mammals, but on two. It's one of the signs by which we as animals hold ourselves superior to the others. To stand on two feet enables the human being to see over things that the four-legged beast cannot. In early times, that gave the human the hunting advantage. Though he or she retains some natural curves in the spine from the old four-legged days, the head is now directly over the tail and the tail over the heels; a more or less vertical line links them all. The crown faces the sky and the eyes gaze at the horizon. It's no accident that vision, in many respects, is the benefit of standing upright.

It is this simple symbol of our being that THE MEDITATION LIFESTYLE is most about. It begins with us relearning the same sense of trust that the little child shows in balancing itself upright for the first time on a ground that is firm and resilient. The spine links earth and sky, and our consciousness moves somewhere between the two of them. And so the book is also about that simple relationship and how completely rewarding it is when we consciously avow that vertical transmission to and fro between the heavy physical world and the airy, light one.

Ancient mythologies, the Egyptian among them, saw creation as being the outcome of a mating process between the same two beings, earth and sky. To be a vertical link between them is thus to embody that union, or to be a son or a daughter of it, a spark of creativity defined only by very existence. To stand on the earth and to link with the heavens expresses readiness to manifest creation in ourselves. It is the simplest posture of our awakened lives. From it comes safety, strength, happiness, richness, the power to give, and all the things that make life worthwhile. From it comes all our aspiration and all our opportunity. Meditation, which we all do, but in which some of us have trained ourselves deliberately and some not, is an exploration of both of those.

To meditate is not necessarily to involve yourself in a complex technique or set of skills, although to do so may be rewarding. It is simply to develop an awareness of the moment, and so to live in and concentrate on that moment, in which life becomes infinitely richer and more comprehensible. Spirituality, someone said, is simply to live with depth. So despite the title of this book, you don't have to be a regular meditator in any school to understand the ideas it contains, or to be 'spiritual' in any conventional sense.

Its basic premise is that meditation is something that comes from the natural awareness of standing on the earth and at the same time being conscious of what we are doing. That is, for me, a spiritual thing but it is not a religious thing – not, at any rate, in the sense we most commonly use that word. Aware standing is about the connection of earth and sky, but it is not about our place in any sort of hierarchy. As the book proceeds, we shall develop a number of very simple practices; if you let them do so, they may change your life.

So you need little or no religion, little or no sense of spirituality, to work with this book, but I cannot guarantee you will not develop a spirituality – in the very broad sense that I use that word – as you read it. To put it another way, you will start to access a larger consciousness than you do at present, not just for some select minutes, but all the time you are awake on earth. It is part of the richness on offer with meditation!

How to Use this Book

This book thus develops the premise that meditation is (or at least can be) a constant activity, not just one to be engaged in as a special practice before or after the busy day. It contains plenty of exercises and practices, but they are deliberately set out so that you find them along the way — as in life! I hope that it therefore encourages you to develop your own exercises, too. Don't feel you need to take the chapters in any order: read the book at whatever pace you like; stop and do an exercise, read it through and see how it feels just to consider it, or mark it as one to do later. Jump to a chapter you like the sound of.

If you're a beginner in meditation, you may still want to start at the front, but fairly soon decide to leap right through to the final chapter, 'Meditation ... is Easy', and then come back. The whole text is a meditation on meditation, which is why I have not sought to split it up with lots of headings. Each chapter does have a tiny summary in its subheading, however.

There are relatively 'deep' meditations at the end of chapters five and seven, which are probably less suitable for beginners than, for instance, the standing exercise in chapter one. In my view, that will always be the place to start.

Meditation ... is Safety

This chapter is mainly about the experience of standing

THE SAFEST experience you can have on the earth is simply to stand on it. That sounds such a simple thing to say, yet life really is more simple than we often admit. Simplicity is one of the themes of this book.

Sitting and lying down are safe, but in those positions you are going to have a different sort of connection with what is underneath you. Standing, you both trust the earth and explore it, for the reason that you touch it and move on it. If you didn't trust it, you wouldn't take a step. Human beings come and go, but the earth is always there, and its roads lead everywhere – and back to you.

Even if you live somewhere where the

ground occasionally moves, because the tectonic plates are colliding, the earth does not stop producing its bounty. Earth is still there to nourish you after the shocks have died away. It is both strong and regenerative. In a temperate climate, it sees spring come after winter, and summer after spring. If you live in a desert, there are moments when the earth blooms, though they may not be so frequent; the cycle of some of its plants is slower and of others faster. If you live in the tundra, the ice within the earth slows the process of growth and decay hugely; but if you live in a beautiful, intermediate climate the earth is covered in rich green, springing from dark humus, most of the time. In an English Maytime, the richness is prodigious, and in a New England fall, it seems afire.

You get your link with the gentle earth best when your feet are bare and the earth is uncovered by concrete or road material. Then your toes can touch earth, individually; you may even be able to feel blades of grass between them. A little bit of dew on the grass is a thrill at first, but the feet soon warm up. Or maybe the feet are on hot sand, which slightly re-forms to accommodate the shape of your foot: the ball, the outside edge, the round heel. The print you leave behind is not a true foot shape, but a bit like a kidney bean with extra dots for the toes. The heel, above all, connects with the earth, but the other points of contact are like little roots, right down to the toes. Anchor the big toe, and you can spread the five toes out from one another, then plant them in the ground again. You are safe.

A Chinese text from the fourth century BC, the *Zhuangzi*, says, 'The True Man breathes with his heels'.*

To get the full effect of standing on the earth, if you have concrete under your feet, or if you are upstairs, or if anything else that is artificial has come between you and the lovable earth, even a prosthetic limb, then you

*Quoted in Vanda Scaravelli, AWAKENING THE SPINE, second edition, London (Pinter & Martin), 2012

will have to use your imagination a little more than if you are on bare ground, or on a floor of organic material such as wood. You perhaps can imagine roots coming from the points of contact your feet have with the earth, finding cracks in the concrete or holes in the road tarmac and going right into the ground beneath.

I used the words 'lovable earth' because you use your feelings when you engage with the earth. You are not shut off from your imagination or from your emotions. Safety is something you *feel*.

If you cannot stand as firmly on the earth as you would like, through injury, take the consciousness of standing firm on the ground and let your imagination override your natural sense-impressions. Or if you cannot find natural earth or wood to stand on, go so far as to imagine that far from being on the thirteenth floor of wherever, you are on the ground in a place you specially love – somewhere you can readily conjure up in your memory, somewhere you easily feel at home. The places you love are generally ones that seem to protect you. The contact with the earth always has hidden within it just a hint of the safety of the womb.

*

Loosen your knees if you possibly can. Some people have never tightened them anyway, but for others loosening them is hard. Try, however difficult it is. You simply need to bring the knees and the shinbones forward so that they are not locked back behind the line of the heels. It will feel as though they are bent, and they indeed need to be for a while in order to break the habit; you are actually over-correcting. Sooner than you think, it will start to feel natural.

After some time of practice in loosening the knees, you will be able to lengthen up the thighbone – as though it is lifting away from the knee joint and into the hip, at the same time as the feet spread down into the ground. This will make the ankle joint work more to support you and the shinbone will engage the strong postural muscles in the calves.

What you are trying to correct is something

that keeps you from really feeling the earth under you in a useful way. If you stiffen your knees, then part of you is resisting this contact with the earth. Loose knees are live knees! But there's another gain, and it's an issue of trust. Think of the earth carrying your weight. It's the earth's job! – but if you stiffen your knees you are saying you have to prop up the whole weight of your body by yourself. You don't. Just like you don't have to carry heavy suitcases but can run them on wheels, so you don't have to carry the whole of your own weight. The ground carries both.

It's possible that the reason for stiffening your knees may have to do with psychology. Don't be alarmed! It may just be that the birth experience was traumatic for you, the opposite of what I suggested in the introduction. If so, locking yourself away from the ground may be something you have to release through bringing unconscious issues into conscious awareness and release. The sense of the earth's protection will then be something you find rather than access at once.

It's worth getting your standing right for more reasons than just the immediate exercise. It changes your life. Unlocking your knees also brings vitality. To read more about this, see chapter six, 'Meditation ... is Energy'.

Having loosened the knees even just a little bit, you can move on to the next thing. Relax as far as you can around the girdle of bones at the base of the spine, the pelvis. Afterwards, you can start to think of the upper body.

*

Relaxing around the pelvis isn't always the easiest thing to do. We accumulate tension in that area, and generally can't let it go at once. Make a start, if you wish, at the sacrum bone, the bone at the base of the spine that is shaped a bit like a shield. It's roughly the size of your fist, and if you put your hand behind you, the back of the hand facing the spine, your fist will tend neatly to fit into where the sacrum bone is. As you stand, just think of this bone spreading back. The relaxation begins from here.

If you can get the feeling of the sacrum spreading back, then as you stand, thinking upward from the feet, the head of each femur (the upper leg bones) stands up into the hip joint and the whole pelvis no longer tends to collapse onto the femur. It's this rather subtle movement, almost more of a thought than an action, that gives the greatest release of tension in this area.*

If you've got that, then okay, you're now trusting the earth, properly! Check as often as you like that your knees are loose. Take your

*A yoga teacher friend, Jenny Beeken, who has most generously helped me with this section, reminds me how the movement really arises out of the breath. She writes: 'The whole spine moves with the breath. At the beginning of the inhalation the coccyx (tail bone) lengthens down out of the sacrum. This results in the sacrum releasing its tension and spreading back and slotting more easily into the pelvis. The lumbar spine then lengthens up out of the sacrum, sending a wave of movement all the way through the spine. On the exhalation the neck vertebrae lengthen up out of the upper back, releasing any tightness in the shoulders and upper back.'

mind back, for a moment, to your feet and their connection with the earth. The feeling can be quite enjoyable!

I sometimes think of the huge plinth in the north-west corner of London's Trafalgar Square, set up along with the rest of the square but left empty when the others were adorned with a statue. Today, as part of an ongoing arts project, it carries an exhibit that is changed every few months. How fragile the transient exhibit, how strong the great stone plinth! But that plinth is you – your lower body, principally, holding up the trunk that contains the vital organs and the heart and head that hold your consciousness.

You're safe, and as you breathe you maybe feel your safety nowhere more strongly than at your breastbone. That bone is another shield like the sacrum, but this one protects the heart and lungs. It's the body's own version of the shield carried by the knights of old. Whereas the sacrum shields the lower organs, the breastbone protects the adult heart, the place where all your inner fire is held.

Just as a hot-air balloon is lifted by the fire beneath it, this proud heart can lift the whole core of your being. Remember, it lifts the core of the body, not the outer frame, which is like the strings of the basket and the basket itself. Your upper body doesn't stiffen, but it lifts from within – and the head, like the great balloon filled with air, stays level.

Transformation. Earth, where you began your thoughts, has risen through air, and in the heart it has become fuel for the fire. The upper body has risen too, without stiffening. Let the shoulders relax at the same time as you feel how big the chest cavity has become. The air in the chest has plenty of room. The breath feels good. You are complete like this, and constantly renewing.

Some of this section may have sounded hard to comprehend and execute, but it will really repay the effort you put into understanding the instructions and carrying them out. It's easier from now!

*

When you breathe, within the lungs the breath oxygenates the blood. You are connecting with air. Although you do not normally feel the pumping action of the heart, you know that the heart is first pumping deoxygenated blood into the lungs, and then pumping oxygenated blood into the body. A fiery engine moves the blood. It is no wonder that the heart is so often associated with fire; the healthy heart is full of energy, always. It takes very little effort to see the heart like the fire that lifts the hot-air balloon.

And of course fire gives out heat. The more present you are in your heart, the more you will be aware of the warmth it gives out. The warmth does not circulate back in: it is free giving. It is not just physical warmth, though: with intention behind it, it becomes something else. If you consciously direct your warmth to something or someone, it acquires another name: love. The way that the heart gives out warmth, it gives it without expectation of return, and yet it is never depleted. It is a conscious conversion of warmth into love. This is the purest love, the love that comes direct from the heart: warmth not emotion, sensation not intellect.

You are safe when you stand on the earth and are aware. From the trust you draw from the earth comes love. Another way to describe love is giving, wisely but without reserve.

CHAPTER TWO

Meditation ... is Richness

*This is a chapter mainly about the
experience of breathing*

BREATHE. Enjoy the air that you breathe.

Of course you were breathing all the time you were doing the standing exercise in chapter one, consciously or unconsciously. There is something special about your breath now, though. It's the breath of a being that has found its safety on the earth and is about to find the absolute freedom of the next world 'up': the world of the breath. That's what you're going to explore next – how real this world is, now that you have found it through the safety of being on the earth. You have found it through a consciousness of something within you and an awareness of what is all around you: the earth, the air, and the beauty of the world that is yours to be in. Let your newfound joy in the world outside fill the place inside you like soft breeze coming into a warmed room.

While standing is what best defines human existence, breath is what turns the standing body into a dynamic being. A body renewed by breath is alive and ready to move. Just stand and breathe and be aware, and you can feel very rich.

We need the ground and what comes from it, and we also need the air, and with it the light. Most of our food comes from the earth – all of it, except the vitamins we derive from sunlight only. So basic are our relationships with the earth and the air that ancient yoga teachings call the physical body the food body. However, they also identify a breath body, which is the one that needs not so much physical food as the air we breathe. There is nothing weird or 'new-agey' about calling something the breath body just because it is a little more conceptual than substantial; giving it this name is simply a way of bringing under one title the many rich forms of awareness that go with breathing. I do take the concept, however, from the anatomy system yoga uses, where the breath body is known as *prana maya kosa*. The Jewish Cabala system, where *ruach* is breath, has a similar concept.

When you eat, you are strongly aware of your physical body. When you breathe, you can be just as aware, with no special information but using a little imagination, of your breath body. Meditation begins in awareness of the connection between the physical body and the breath body.

The breath occupies the place in you that you created by standing on the earth and trusting it, the place that is really your core. That done, you not only allowed your upper body to lift from the heart or 'core', but by trusting the earth and relaxing at the base of the spine you created more space for the lower organs, and thus more space for the lungs. So your breath is potentially bigger for the fact that you relaxed your lower body. You've also allowed your upper body to lift: not by tensing it, but by feeling the heart rising while the shoulders relaxed down. Both practices made more room for the lungs.

Think of how, if you were supported by two friendly hands that cupped the back of your head, your whole spine could hang downwards from the top. It would do this like a string of beads, each vertebra separating a little more from the last, until you reached the sacrum and the coccyx. They reach downward into the earth, just like a spade that goes cleanly in. When you've done this, take your awareness back to your heart and lungs.

*

The breath is the place we come to and come back to endlessly when we meditate. It is the bridge between a world we can see with our physical eyes and one that we sense when our eyes are closed or their focus is softened but we remain aware. It's the place where we can rest for a moment, the junction of consciousness. Imagine now that when you do not much feel your physical body but are aware of breathing, the very breath both fills you and clothes you. Now you may *feel* what I have been describing: that's your breath body.

Let me repeat that far from being a remote concept, the breath body is just a name for a real state of consciousness. You enter it when you are happy in nature and the sun is shining and nothing much seems to matter beyond the sound of the birds, the sunlight at your back and brightening the way ahead. You may never want to call it the breath body, but it's easy to recognize at these moments that there is something bodylike that is different from the heavy one you carry around and notice most when you go uphill or downhill. Yet you enter the happy consciousness of the breath body all the more easily because on your hike or your country walk your feet are constantly touching the ground. They give you the trust that lets you open to the air and the light.

The contact with the earth is real. Instead

of that 'breath-body world' being nebulous, as it might be if you began in mid-air, it is real like the earth, precisely because you rise into it through the strong link you are making with the earth. Only it isn't such an effort to keep in good repair as the physical body is.

I had the experience that leads me to say this when walking mountain ridges in Bulgaria, not very long ago. Every footfall was a reminder of the ground beneath me, yet my consciousness seemed to be aware of something more subtle and more lovely even than the views I was enjoying – which at one time extended across three countries: Bulgaria, Greece and Macedonia. It came to me that all you need to do to live in a higher consciousness is to stand on the earth and be happy.

Walking is one of the best ways to become familiar with the breath body. First, in walking you need slightly more breath than in standing – indeed quite a lot more when you are going uphill. More importantly, as you walk you engage your feet with the earth in a way that releases energy. As the heel comes down, even if it is not in time with your breath, it follows a rhythm like the breath. As you walk through, your foot goes through a complete movement, ending in the little spring that propels you forward and into the next step.

Breath is like that: a moment of placement and a moment of springing onward. Yet we don't hold the tension in our feet that we often do in our diaphragms. The best step is barefoot, and the better the step, the better the breath. Hard surfaces and stiff shoes are equally limiting to the foot and to the breath.

Your friends would be surprised to hear how familiar you have become with what to some spiritual people is known as the 'etheric body'.

*

Richness comes when we feel each breath from inside our bodies. That doesn't mean being self-conscious about our breath. I went through agonies as a child because when I was being taught to sing I managed to get the impression that the breath was a conscious, complex effort involving a detailed knowledge of the muscles involved. Actually, breathing in ordinary life, and certainly in meditation, is completely allied to relaxation; the more relaxed you are, the less self-conscious, the better you breathe.

You can't be taught to breathe, because the breath is yours – yours to enjoy and to discover. The only hints that I can usefully give are those that remind you what you have to *unlearn*. Among the things to unlearn, the principal one is the belief that you actively *take* a breath. There may be good reasons for taking a breath, special occasions as it were, but you do not need to do so in any part of your normal routine. The breath takes itself when you relax at the end of an outbreath. For on all but the special occasions, any muscles you have around your diaphragm and lungs are used to get rid of the old breath, not take the new. The new breath is just what happens when, having used those muscles, you relax or allow.

The breath is worth watching, but only to enjoy what is happening, not to analyse or alter it. Vanda Scaravelli says, 'Receive the air in a passive, detached way, as though you were only an observer, an outsider'.* She uses the beautiful image of mist spreading into a tree-filled valley for how the lungs receive the breath. I don't think her gentle statement rules out the emotion of happiness, a sort of greeting to the new breath, a recognition that in taking it we choose to continue our lives rather than stop. When we expel the old breath it is not the end of ourselves, just the end of a tiny moment of life, and it's worth watching the breath to the end. To do so means we extract every bit of value from it, and to see it to the end gives closure on that single rich moment.

The new moment is sweet, it is full of expectation. Even when enormous fears have been grabbing us, there is still the opportunity to extract one moment of joy, one tiny moment now. This breath-moment offers no

*AWAKENING THE SPINE, p. 174

statement about the next moment, or the previous one: it is just itself. While impossible burdens are piling upon us, this one moment can be welcomed, can still be good. It fills us as the breath fills us, and when we have used the breath, we watch it leave us. Who can say the next breath will not be equally sweet?

One meditation technique is to regard every breath we take as a meditation in itself. It's a nice answer for the stern teacher (probably the one inside us) that says, 'Have you meditated this morning?'. 'Yes', you can answer, 'Ten thousand times'! The meditation within the breath consists of being absolutely present with the breath as it enters, maybe even visualizing it as light entering the system. It fills you, your being becoming light, until for a tiny interval there is a standing still, like the moment at the top of the wave before it breaks. That is the climax, but not the end of your meditation; that is the moment when, full of light, you are aware of being part of all life. The climax, but not the end, for as the breath leaves you, you can see every cell of your body filling with light and your whole body radiating it. By the time you have emptied your lungs, that light has gone forth, richly, to all your environment, other human beings included. Then comes the moment of completion – another brief, brief time of standing still – before you gladly relax into the next breath.*

A fuller way in which you can use the single breath as a meditation is to imagine the whole season of the year on every breath. Thus as you relax into the inbreath, feel as though the first flowers of spring are all around, opening as the sun shines on them. For me and for many in Britain that will be a vision of golden daffodils, but it will vary with how your seasons manifest in your part of the world. As you draw the full breath, feel summer breaking out into full splendour: a rich abundance of

*Another book by Jenny Beeken is really helpful with the breath: DON'T HOLD YOUR BREATH. London (Polair), 2004

leaves, flowers, trees and a mass of colour and light. After the tiny moment of stillness when the breath peaks, you have the time of harvest, turning into autumn in Britain, fall in the United States. Then, the lungs finally emptying, you have winter: maybe cold and unattractive, but the joy of winter is the knowledge that it is lit from within by the new season – or breath – of which it contains the promise. And the new breath comes like spring: not striven for, a sudden awakening.

Notice, whether you do the simple one-breath meditation or the rather fuller version of the preceding paragraph, how when you are filled with light, you give naturally of that light. Consciously feel yourself shining. The light cannot help but emanate from you. You are lit like a star or a sun, and there is nothing that stars can do but shine.

CHAPTER THREE

Meditation ... is Strength

Standing strong brings both vision and gentleness

REMEMBER the plinth in Trafalgar Square I mentioned in chapter one, the one that is so massive? The artist Antony Gormley, who also created the Angel of the North outside Newcastle-upon-Tyne, had 2400 people in turn stand on the plinth for an hour. It was his own response to the ongoing challenge artists had been set of what to put on the plinth.

What a symbol of strength something can be whose base is cut on four right angles, whose mass is so great and so rectilinear! The cube is the most basic figure of strength, built on exact and equal measurements. This plinth is not a cube, but as strong, almost. It would take a massive statue indeed to dwarf this plinth.

In nature, the commonest symbol of strength is less often the cube than the mountain. In meditation we may use the mountain to give a sense of aspiration, of our rising above the plains, but let us stay for the moment with the mountain's own strength. Its base is always much larger than its apex: the mountain's feet are surrounded by a vast skirt, tapering away into plains or other mountains. No earthquake will topple it. So strong is it indeed that it rises higher into the sky than any other object connected to the earth can go.

The other great attribute of a mountain is stillness. At its base it inspires silent awe, and its top is so far above the din of city and plain that it is invariably silent. It is its own silence, but its quality is modesty, and silence its reward. As one of the earliest books of wisdom says, the stillness of the mountain is perfectly self-contained. It does not need to look beyond itself, even though mountains connect well with each other by ridges and cols.*

As you place your feet on the earth, in your strength you can be like a mountain. Standing as described, you can be silent – modest, too

* The image of the single mountain is derived from Hexagram 52 of the I Ching, or 'Book of Changes'. The Willhelm/Jung translation reads:

'The image of this hexagram is the mountain, the younger son of heaven and earth. The male principle is at the top, because it strives upward by nature; the female principle is below, since the direction of its movement is downward. Thus there is rest because the movement has come to its normal end.

'In its application to man, the hexagram turns upon the problem of achieving a quiet heart. It is very difficult to bring quiet to the heart. While Buddhism strives for rest through an ebbing away of all movement in nirvana, the Book of Changes holds that rest is merely a state of polarity that always posits movement as its complement. Possibly the words of the text embody directions for the practice of yoga.'

– and yet your vision reaches beyond all other parts of the landscape. Once again, the strength of your standing begins in your feet, and your strength is greatest when the consciousness is in the heart, for then you are in touch with a fire that radiates not only love, but strength. The mountain consciousness is worth a meditation in itself, whether you prefer to sit or stand.

*

Another quality that comes from this mountain image is gentleness. For all its strength, the slopes of the mountain are home to streams that take water down its sides, water that perhaps dances in sunlight. High up, the rocks of the mountain may be gently overlaid with new-fallen snow, its crystals forming a blanket of gentle quiet over shapes that would otherwise be jagged. Each one of the flakes is a fragile six-pointed star shape, until thawing and refreezing brings new stability to the blanket of snow.

It is one of life's seeming contradictions, but not really a contradiction at all, that out of strength comes gentleness. The one of us that is strong has really no need to demonstrate strength: his or her strength is known. It is the weaker being that constantly needs to prove itself by actions of apparent strength, even violence. Meditation, when it begins with trust in the earth beneath us, when it explores the safety of every individual moment of life, actually brings strength – for all that many associate it with developing sensitivity. Properly, I like to think via the equations:

$$MEDITATION = STRENGTH$$
$$STRENGTH = GENTLENESS$$
$$GENTLENESS = SENSITIVITY.$$

That way, the sensitivity is not an unprotected, nervous sensitivity, but one that is created in poise and balance.

My aunt, who was also a meditation teacher, liked to think of the standing posture as one in which by our very awareness linked earth with the Pole Star above, a vertical rod or chain of light. She had wonderful poise herself, not in a 'better-than-you' way, but expressing itself in natural serenity. At the end of her life, she stared out the fast-advancing form of leukaemia for eighteen months by sheer focus on the light within her.

*

I'd like to suggest that a perfectly natural outcome of real meditation is non-violence. Non-violence begins in the very way we have looked at the breath: no forcing, nothing done to push or to hold. In our standing, we have entirely avoided rigidity. The looseness in our knees, if we can achieve it, makes us equally ready to dance or to move quickly, when we dodge the arrows that spring out from life's confusing patterns. It is unsurprising that the posture is akin to the stances that begin some of the non-aggressive martial arts.

Violence that has accumulated in us through the injustices of life does not necessarily go the minute we start to meditate. We cannot escape looking into ourselves if we are to release it. Interestingly, though, recent neurological research has shown that through meditation we actually grow a part of our brain which helps with this.* It is an astonishing result, because for a long time scientists thought that growing our brains in this way was impossible – that they were 'hard-wired' only to develop in a predetermined way. In fact, a relatively short-term practice of deep meditation has been shown to develop a small area of the brain known as the anterior cingulate. The anterior cingulate, one of the parts of the brain that has formed in the higher animals only, is

* Andrew Newberg, MD and Mark Robert Waldman, HOW GOD CHANGES YOUR BRAIN. New York, NY (Ballantine Books), 2009

the part that controls our response to the 'fight or flight' mechanism that is the animal brain's response to danger. Humans have the option of controlling both flight and fight and offering what we might call a civilized response instead. They thus have the option of staying calm, avoiding a fight and showing their distaste for flight too. To choose the alternatives to violence, positively, is disarming to others and it involves a full engagement of consciousness in this brain area. Yet when you meditate, the anterior cingulate *grows*. You have a heightened ability to return violent anger with a large understanding through your meditation practice.

Yoga, meaning union, is often thought of as a set of postures, known as *asanas*. In fact, the classic texts give eight parts or 'Limbs' to the practice of yoga, with the *asanas* as the fifth of these – a body-quietening prelude to the practice of meditation (which itself has three stages to it). The first two of the Limbs are concerned with ethical choices in the broadest sense of that word. One of them is a quality we have just mentioned, *svhadyaya*, self-study. It is also from this two-thousand-year-old wisdom that Gandhi took the principle of *ahimsa*, non-violence. Here is our modern yoga teacher, Jenny Beeken, writing about *ahimsa*:

'The wider, broader meaning of the word *ahimsa* is "love embracing all", seeing ourselves and our fellow human beings and all creation as part of the whole, part of us – so loving all, that the destruction of any part of the earth or creation is the destruction of ourselves. So "non-violence" encompasses seeing into all things with love, creating and affirming peace everywhere, knowing that that which manifests as violence only comes out of fear. If we can see through the fear and just love – whoever, wherever, whatever – then we in our hearts are practising *ahimsa* – non-violence.

'We may possibly look at the word "non-violence" and say "yes, I believe in this", and then look at the world around us and say "how terrible the violence is that manifests there – what on earth can we do about it?". Mahatma

Gandhi, the world's greatest exponent of non-violence, said: "Look to yourselves, to the violence which manifests within yourself". It may be a shock to feel that we could have feelings of anger or violence hidden within us, yet look at the little ways it can come out unexpectedly in each one!'*

The strength that comes through meditation is not a strength that complicates our relationships with others. Rather, through a feeling of strength within, we feel the gentle giant – the one who no longer has the slightest need to harm anyone. It may take a bit of practice.

*

Just as Gandhi's practice of *ahimsa* proved to the world that meekness is not weakness, so (I'd like to suggest) the connection with inner experience that we make in meditation makes us anything but ineffective. Most of postmodern society is fixated on the clock. It reminds us that time is money, it throws deadlines at

*Jenny Beeken, ANCIENT WISDOM. London (Polair), 2007, p. 11

us, and we tend to regard it as the best that can be when things go 'like clockwork'. Great!

Except that things going 'like clockwork' makes it sound as though the highest quality of life we can have occurs when things are easy. Most of us would prefer to say that we feel 'at the height' in the extremes of life. 'Like clockwork' is lovely, but I think we'd soon get bored of it! In its response to the rather shallow set of values I'd call the clockwork ones, meditation is actually deeply subversive. I sometimes think of living in the moment as the most subversive thing we can do in the postmodern world. Instead of the fixation with the passing of time and the sensation that life is no more than a struggle against a hostile progress of moments, meditation takes just one moment at a time and offers that single moment as complete, infinitely rich and ultimately fulfilling.

The more we practise, the richer the moment can be. Linear time is utterly meaningless within this awareness. The one moment is all that will ever matter – and the next moment is born of it but in total novelty. And joy, if we allow that.

When I was a child, time seemed to pass much slower than it does now. To the best of my knowledge, this was not because my brain was younger, but because I was distracted for less of the time. Modern life says: 'Listen to me!' … 'No, listen to *me*!' … 'No, listen to *meee*!' In meditation and its accompanying lifestyle we listen, but what we hear is within us, and what goes on around us is just *there*, not demandingly there. So the moment in meditation lasts forever, but the moment in ordinary life gets shorter and shorter with every new dependency we succumb to. Those who feel most overburdened may be those who have allowed each moment to shrink until it is not noticeable. For the values of life, therefore, this sort of meditation is a recovery process, and takes almost no time at all.

CHAPTER FOUR

Meditation ... is Beauty

Mainly about the imagination

HERE'S another exercise. First, remembering how you stood in the first chapter, do the same now. Refer back if you need to, but maybe you are now getting used to practising it. Once it becomes familiar, this exercise gets easier to remember and do. Your knees are more used to not locking, and you tend to feel the relaxation around the pelvic area and the good placing of the feet from the moment you loosen the knees. If you're less practised, keep to the discipline of working upwards from the ground: first the placing of the feet, then the loosening of the knees, then the gentle sense of expansion around the pelvis. Remember the adage quoted, that the true man breathes with his heels.

Imagine either that you are on a beach, your feet on soft sand, your gaze extending out across the water to the horizon, or else that you are standing on some outcrop of rock, high up, breathing cool fresh air, and looking out over the plain or the valley below you. Maybe the sun is just coming over the horizon, or just setting.

Whichever scene you prefer, let the colours

affect you: the soft blues and perhaps the turquoise and even rosy pink colours over the sea, or the greens and lavenders and blues of the landscape, or maybe the rich ochres of sandstone. The colours are your peace, and the sheer beauty of them will help your upper body to lift, from the heart or from the breastbone that shields it, breathing more cleanly, more enjoyably.

There is contentment in breathing, in the balance between the outbreath and the in-breath, and a contentment in the gentle rhythm that the breath observes. Contentment is itself another quality from those first two Limbs of yoga, where it is identified by the Sanskrit word *santosa*. Standing on your beach, in the warmth of the sun, you maybe know contentment.

*

Note that there is a you that is breathing, and a you that can watch you breathing. Try and become aware of that second you, the watching one. It gets to know the movements your chest makes with the breath; it gets to recognize the difference between the inbreath and the outbreath; it gets to be aware even of the tiny pause at the end of the breath, the moment when you allow another breath to enter, just by relaxing and letting the vacuum fill. It's the one that feels the joy of doing that.

Stay doing that watching, contentedly enjoying each breath and the choice that leads you into each new breath.

After a while, see if you can even notice a you that is watching the you that is watching. Perhaps that sounds strange – if it does, read the sentence again and try to take in what I'm saying with your imagination, not your reasoning mind. Can you observe the observer? It can be done. It may take many times of practice before this you feels real, yet in time it may become more real than the other yous. It demands patience. But as you keep on with it, the awareness grows and continues growing.

One thing that may start to come is a sense that this you, the one that is watching the watcher, has no boundaries, a freedom to be wherever it is, and with that a sense that at this level of freedom there is light rather than form. With this self you live in light. In your imagination, let the light shine from this self into the watching self. Love it in so doing. Love it as it feels joy at the moment of the new breath, but love it as it feels pain too. That watching self takes enough criticism from other people, it is really gratifying for it to feel loved. Never be critical of it yourself; it is your feeling body and it will lead you towards good things when you love it, and it will just curl up if you are angry with it. Love it whatever; it tries!

Now let the same light flood through that watching self and reach even the breathing self. Let it reach the tension that that breathing, body self often feels; let it reach any pain, let it soften any stiffness. You can even feel the light extending beyond it, penetrating the

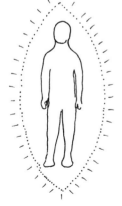

earth beneath and reaching up above you.

Now you have a beautiful picture of a you that is both full of light and surrounded by light. If you are aware of it, with what sense do you feel it? Touch, as a spatial sense? Can you see it, even? You may naturally see it as a traditional aura shape, an oval that is pointed top and bottom, known as a vesica. It gracefully enfolds you.

*

As an alternative, see it as a six-pointed star, all around you, because then you have the symbol we looked at for a moment in the last chapter. As I said, when you properly imagine a star it really shines. It is not just a piece of geometry. It is a shining light-source, centred in your heart. When you are really used to seeing this star, when you are really used to being this star, you can even use it as a way of moving out of the normal awareness of things as separate from you, to bring about a unitary consciousness in which there is no division between subject and object (for more on this, see pp 84–5).

The bottom point of the star goes down into the earth; the top point reaches up above, and the whole star blazes with light.* The centre is roughly at your heart. Feel how the action of the heart, which is a natural pump

*Cf p. 47n on the mountain as a union of opposites.

anyway, gives you a clue as to how the blazing light is constantly replenished. Not just constantly but perpetually; there is no death in this image. At the physical-body level, though – just as through the workings of the lungs and heart, the blood is oxygenated and the body refreshed. Only this light shines out beyond you: it shines endlessly into the distance, and everything around you is illuminated.

Every cell of your body fills with light, but so does everybody you think of 'in this light' – every thing, too.

*

It's a common misapprehension about meditation that in it you have to turn off both the mind and the feelings. In fact, both are used in meditation, but it is important that neither is in a position to dominate you. In this book, you may have noticed how often I have used the body, not the mind, as a way into a meditative state. You examine how you feel with your body, and from that move into a mental process which has much more to do with the imagination than either the reasoning or the worrying mind. The feelings are actually rather important in meditation, so long as they support you. Thus in chapter one we talked about the feeling of safety. The appreciation of beauty is another – especially if it is not so much an intellectual aesthetic you are following, as simple delight or a feeling of being moved by something beautiful.

Sometimes, I like to explore these feelings from the standing posture which by now must be familiar to you. Having found and experienced it just for what it is, I will then use my arms to explore simple positive emotions.

First, I throw them up above my head, reaching as it were for the sky. I then explore what feeling has come out of that arm position. I don't want to limit the feeling either for you, the reader, or any class I might be working with, but let's suggest that one feeling that might be felt is exultation. Next, I bring them down and equally gently I fling them out to the sides, straight out from the shoulders, palms upwards, where they may either catch the sunlight or maybe hold something up. I feel, again, what goes with this.

I hope that it's starting to become clear how each posture carries a feeling. From the 'outstretched' position I next bring the hands forward, elbows out, to form a circle – fingers touching in front – and then bring them in to my heart. This is one of the most evocative of the movements. It is difficult not to imagine it in some way bringing out our sympathies. The next is more subtle: I drop my hands to the sides, but then open the palms out. See what this one encourages you to feel! I've heard many students give different answers, but one thing I am certain of is that there is a lovely gentleness involved in this one.

Lastly, I return my arms to my sides, palms inwards as they were before I began, but now even that posture has some sort of feeling with it – maybe just a feeling of simplicity.

*

Let's move to something else that evokes feel-ings. For this, you can sit or even lie down. You can enjoy the sunshine, with your imagination. The teacher White Eagle, whom I have followed all my life, says in his little book THE QUIET MIND:

'If things do not happen as you want them to happen, know that a better way is being found. Trust, and never forget that the true way is the way of love. Flowers do not force their way with great strife. Flowers open to perfection slowly in the sun.'*

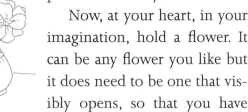

Now, at your heart, in your imagination, hold a flower. It can be any flower you like but it does need to be one that visibly opens, so that you have that feeling within yourself, at the place you are holding the flower, your heart centre. It may be a wildflower, a round chrysanthemum with many petals, or a simple daisy; for many, it will immediately be a rose. Think, with the rose, how strong the stem is, and even of the thorns that protect it – but come back always

*White Eagle, THE QUIET MIND. Liss, Hampshire (White Eagle Publishing Trust), 1998, p. 59

to the serenity of the flower itself and its infinitely gentle perfume. See how every cell of
every petal can catch the light.

All that you are doing in this little meditation exercise is feeling the warmth of the sun
upon your heart. It brings safety, a safety in
which you can imaginatively unfold the creative being that you are. Warmed by the sun,
your heart is a place of giving and a place of
creativity. There is even a fire inside it, as the
warmth really starts to take effect.

Relax. Go through this exercise at other
times, as many times indeed as you can remember to do it. At the end, imagine if you
like that you lie down on the grassy bank in
perfect rest. You may awake later to the vision
of flowers all around you. Contentment, again.

As humans we are quite able to be terrified
of contentment. We feel that the moment we
let everything go, we shall lose control. People
sometimes resist meditation because having a
difficult life has become a drug in itself, and
to change life's parameters feels anything but

safe. That's why in my teaching I like to begin with the ground beneath us offering deep
safety. We need not fear contentment. At the
moment beauty breathes into us the great perfume of contentment, we are actually 'saved',
because beauty is uplifting, and even redeem-
ing. *Santosa*, or contentment, is a place you can
find again and again in meditation.

*

Perfect relaxation is hard for us because it is
part of the human condition constantly to
strive, and not to strive can itself be stressful,
because it feels like non-achievement. Maybe
to relax and not strive is itself an achievement.

There's a word, 'Faustian', for compulsive
striving. The German poet, Goethe, created a
deeply philosophical vision of the character
he calls 'Faust', driven by an endless, insatiable
passion for new experience. His pact with Mephistopheles, the devil, is that his life will not
end until he finds something so compelling he
wishes to stay with it. His pact is based on the
fair gamble that this moment will never come.

Yet it does. For Faust, the all-satisfying moment is strangely philanthropic; it is when he decides to devote himself to creating a paradise for others. Suddenly, there is perception of things way beyond himself: human need, idealism, beauty, created paradise. The human spirit is here aspiring, not vainly searching. In this moment, there is reason to say, as we must always say in meditation: 'It is okay to be *right here*'.

What Faust actually says is: '*Werweile doch, du bist so schön!*': 'Linger awhile, thou art so fair' in the translation I once studied. Faust loses his gamble with Mephistopheles, and seemingly abandons himself to hell forever more. Goethe, however, is an enlightened teacher, and he knows better than to let our contentment be the moment we go to hell. Hell's angels gather round, singing triumphantly of Faust's damnation. But another chorus unexpectedly appears, angels of eternal light and love. Their reminder is that aspiration to the Source of Being leads unerringly to that Source, and that no amount of distraction can shake it. Their words, here translated into

English, have some relevance for the meditator:

> *What is not part of you,*
> *You need not share it:*
> *What inwardly troubles you,*
> *You need not bear it....*
> *Only the loving, Love*
> *Guides to its source!*

In the final scene, Faust is carried up to higher and higher planes of bliss, just as people sometimes experience in meditation. The very final chorus (set sublimely by both Schumann and Mahler) makes the feminine the principle that reunites us in Oneness.

> *All of the transient*
> *Is parable, only:*
> *The insufficient*
> *Here grows to reality:*
> *The indescribable*
> *Here is done:*
> *Woman, eternal,*
> *Beckons us on.*

Meditation is not always ecstatic, but it can be.

CHAPTER FIVE

Meditation ... is Happiness

*What we find in meditation
goes right on through our lives*

THE IMAGE of the bank of flowers is also one of indescribable happiness. As I write this part of the book, I am looking out over a garden with Tuscan hills beyond it. This morning, it's not even sunny, and yet as I gaze my heart

opens at the sight of the cypresses that stand out from the undulating landscape and remind me where I am. It is spring, and the landscape is full of greenness – from the bright green grass to the dark green of the cypresses and the grey-green of the olive trees. The predominating colour of the flowers, by contrast, is soft mauve: in the lilac, in the wisteria, in many of the irises. Tuscany is many an English person's definition of happiness, and artists, intellectuals and tourists alike have flooded here from England and from America, believing that Tuscan light will bring them a completer joy than they can find in their everyday lives.

Actually, the practice of meditation helps us find happiness in our everyday lives wherever they are lived. Tuscany is a symbol of happiness, not a requirement before we have it. Happiness is something we often think of as quite an elusive quality, but it is to be seen in the human face in two quite different but classic moments. One is the light that we see in a baby's eyes when it smiles: a natural, instinctive happiness that may infect us too. We look into those eyes and cannot imagine that one who knows so little of life could look so full of beauty, love and happiness. Sometimes people shrug and say, 'Thank goodness this little one does not know what life has in store for it!'.

In fact, the other time we see happiness in the human face is in the maybe wrinkled face of someone who has been through a vast calendar of human experience, and won their way through to the end, maybe in advanced age. It is the happiness of wisdom and it may also be the happiness of knowing that the way back to bliss is to turn our sight to the same kingdom that showed in the baby's eyes, the sense of where it came from. Is that suggestion too religious, too spiritual? I am not sure I can avoid saying it. Even as I write, with lovely synchronicity, a friend has just called me over to show me a book of colour photographs, and in particular one of a wrinkled peasant woman, her eyes just dancing with joy even as her wrinkles speak of toil.

Meditation does not value life over death but visits both equally. In the very moment of the breath, meditation leads us into the fullness of life and at the close of each breath it teaches us how to die. Each new breath is a new incarnation, a new moment to be experienced fully and maybe joyfully. But the cycle, every time, moves through to emptiness – if only to empty lungs, ready to be filled again – something I shall return to in chapter eight.

Emptiness is a word often used in meditation, and in Buddhist meditation particularly. (The terms I've used so far have been from the yoga tradition, rather than the Buddhist.) There it often means an absence of expectation, an escape from the will, a total waiting. In a connected way, writers today refer to 'emptiness' as useful in the realm of problem-solving: to be empty of solutions is to be ready for them to grow, whereas to be full of them is to be ready for chaos.* To many poets, night is a time for creativity.

I'd prefer, at this moment, to quote my own teacher, White Eagle, again. The passage takes up a theme already embarked upon here, a theme of three different selves or levels of life. The word he uses for emptiness is actually 'blankness', or maybe 'nothingness'. In the following passage, if you find the word 'soul' difficult, what he is describing is simply the part of you that receives all the sense-impressions, happy and painful, the one that watches the breath (see chapter four). White Eagle says:

*On emptiness and chaos, see M. Scott Peck, A DIFFER-ENT DRUM. London (Arrow Books), 1990, chapter five

'Endeavour to find yourself, the real "I", beneath the outer coats of flesh and mind which obscure it. To do this try to think in terms of three; first, think of the ordinary person that you are in daily life; next, think about the soul, known only to yourself (or so you think); and thirdly, try to find the place of stillness and quiet at the centre of your being, the real "I".

'As you learn to withdraw into your inner self, the outer self will, as it were, dissolve; and the inner self begin to assert itself. This inner self is a personality, a soul — and a something more. If you will train yourself in contemplation, you will find that beneath the soul there is a place of stillness, of blankness, of nothingness if you like. Yet when you are confronted with the seeming nothingness that lies beneath the conscious self, you will gradually become aware of an all-ness, a sense of affinity with universal life and an at-one-ment with God. In this condition there can be no separation, no darkness, no fear: nothing exists but love and an exquisite joy that permeates your whole being.'*

In meditation, there is a happiness to be found that can be rather greater even than the happiness Tuscan sunlight offers! It is a sense of absolute relation to the whole of the rest of life, undefined in its extent. It can be found in the ways White Eagle describes, both in the image of the unfolding flower and in the process of uncovering what is hidden beneath experience, stripping away each layer of an onion, in the way just described. Guessing, though, that for many this is where meditation seems to become hard, let me offer a couple of gentle techniques.

*

One of these techniques is present in the classic meditation image of the white lotus that floats on the water, the water of life. In meditation, I am often helped by feeling that if I can hold this image, I can find a consciousness

* White Eagle, LIVING WITH LOVE. Liss, Hampshire (WEPT), 2007, pp. 36–37

that is not easily found outright. Let's explain. I think first of the water and its maybe murky, but deeply nutritious, depths – from which the lotus, or lily, draws what it needs to grow. As the meditation unfolds, I will locate my breathing in this image of the water, too, for however still is the surface of the water there will always be currents in its depths. The moving depth is like my breath, always there, just beneath the surface of consciousness. Through this image, I can be aware of my breath without the breath intruding into other areas that I want my consciousness to explore.

One of these places is the lotus itself, but another is the sky. I have a need to feel the beauty of the vast heavens just as much as I want to feel how nutritious is the water and the mud. The gentleness of the sky is part of my restfulness, and from it comes the light.

The lotus, though, rests neither in the air nor deep in the water, but right on its still surface. Sometimes, before I even begin to use the image of the lotus, I can free myself from my

The floating lotus. Technically, the Indian or Chinese lotus does not float but rises above the water. The western water lily, shown here, floats. I love to use the sense of floating, because it is the most free of effort, the image most free of desire, that I can imagine. I have treated it as white but water lilies can be a beautiful bright magenta pink too and the lotus is often blue — as it was to the ancient Egyptians.

mind's prison just by seeing, and then imagining that I am part of the light dancing on the water's surface. Water has its dimensions, the sky has its dimensions, and yet the dancing light has no thickness at all and no breadth that we could measure, for it never stays the same.

In that dancing light I can immerse myself in real joy, a joy beyond what the mind can ever offer in its usual workings.

Generally, though, and following the tradition of many meditators, I go further than this, and use the image of the lotus itself. That floats on the water too, but it has also to it a beauty of form, a purity of colour, and an intricacy of structure when we start to look at every cell of its white petals. And it has a golden heart: a heart in which in imagination we can lose ourselves, a heart in which there can be nothing but golden light. Nothing but golden light, truly — and yet we are there ourselves, in this light. We are lost, absorbed, dissolved in light.

This is the moment when, traditionally, we begin to witness the famous jewel in the heart of the lotus. Within the golden light, form (which we thought we had lost) appears. The jewel is universal but it is also an image of the greatest self we can be, each facet carefully cut by experience in life. The jewel is both us and everything, and in its shining light there is total happiness. Every facet reflects light, one after another sparkling in turn, in a random dance. There is ecstasy in every detail of the vision.

Sheer beauty has taken me out of the limitations of my mind. Sheer beauty enthralls me now.

*

Another way I reach into a higher happiness, a happiness not located in narrow self, is to use the classic stages of meditation that are given to us by the Eight Limbs of Yoga.* Limb number three, we may remember, is taken up by the *asanas*, the postures of yoga. After that Limb and two more (breathing, and control of the senses), we move into the stages of meditation itself, three of them, each with a Sanskrit name.

The first, *dharana*, normally translates as 'concentration'. By definition, concentration involves one object only. In another context we might concentrate more generally – on our work or on what we are saying – but in meditation there is normally just one object

*see above, p. 52

for concentration. It might be a flower such as we have already enjoyed, or the lotus of this very section; or it might be the flame of a candle, carefully left to become still with our deepening concentration. There are types of meditation that focus at this point on an image of a great being or teacher, such as the Buddha or Jesus, the Christ, and others that concentrate attention upon the breath rhythms even more than I have suggested so far. Sometimes, it works when with eyes still open we gaze at a single blank point on the opposite wall.

What matters above all is that there is only one point, one image for concentration. Our point of concentration must hold us, not distract us with its many facets. And so we stay, as long as we feel the need and the ability, gazing with inward or even outer eyes, at the single point or object.

The next Limb of yoga, number seven, is *dhyana*. I like to translate this as 'contemplation' but all the English words we use are confusing. There is a very different idea in Buddhism also generally referred to as 'contemplation'. Where in concentration we held ourselves to one object or point, in *dhyana* we draw into our consciouness absolutely everything around us. Contemplation gives an opportunity early in our meditation to bring into our awareness all that is present with us and not be distracted by it, be it furniture in the room, distant noises outside, a vase of flowers, or other people in the meditating group. But at this deeper stage, where it follows concentration, it is a joyful absorption of all things, a sense that there is no separation, no limitation, to consciousness. It is a moment when the whole of life seems perfectly crafted and formed.

Both concentration and contemplation, *dharana* and *dhyana*, offer deep happiness. There is a whole level of happiness yet to be discovered, though, beyond this point. As we saw, *dharana*, concentration, like a line leading away from us, is a total focus on one thing, in which nothing else seems to have any validity whatsoever. *Dhyana*, what I call contemplation but others may call absorption, is the total opposite. In *dhyana*, everything is present, everything matters, but everything matters equally. Nothing dominates or disturbs. The world and its beauties stretch out on either side of us. The world is full of joy, expressed in an infinite variety of forms. Somewhere we would if we could take every one of them to the source of life, in blessing and love.

*

How can we be in both states of mind, concentration and contemplation, simultaneously, when they are virtual opposites of each other? The answer is that we can't. Concentration, focus on one thing, cannot be had at exactly the same time as a mental awareness of the equal importance of every little thing we could ever conceive. The mind, unable to take us further, absents itself.

If we remain alert and aware at this point, something extraordinary happens to our consciousness. We retain the sensation of concentrating and we retain the sensation of contemplating, but in the paradox that cannot be resolved we have something beyond what mind can offer us. We have concentration, we have contemplation or absorption, but we have nothing we can any longer see. We have objectless concentration. Not only are the objects we once valued gone, we have no sense of ourselves as subjects and of the things we have been gazing at as objects. Our minds have retreated, and our meditation has led us into a place that allows us to experience oneness: no subject and no object. All one.

This state has a Sanskrit word to describe it too. It is *samadhi*, often translated as 'bliss'. I prefer to retain the phrase 'objectless concentration', and whether that is or is not a perfect translation, it is a common one. It is in this state of objectless concentration that we experience bliss. Here, in the moment when there is no subject and no object there is only experience of being. It is light, it is utterly joyful, it is completely free.

Sometimes, in this state, I believe we go on

to have other experiences and visions. I believe it is because we have got to a point, a level of consciousness, where there can be form
and there can be not form, interchangeably.
We see things, but without a sense of separation from them. What is quite certain is that
it is not the will that drives us any longer, nor
is it the mind. It is happiness that leads us, a
spontaneous awareness and experience of life
in a no-longer-physical but very real form. It's
maybe what meditation is all about.

CHAPTER SIX

Meditation ... is Energy

Meditating on the hoof

IN SOCIETY, meditators have a curious, and not entirely consistent, profile. There's the image of the meditator as someone rather out of touch with life, a little vague even. Young and wide-eyed, or older, bearded and sandalled. There's a counter-image that has sometimes been carefully fostered: the businessman in lotus posture. Transcendental Meditation (TM) has advertised itself in this way, not infrequently. Sometimes meditators are seen as out of spiritual reach, but at others they are viewed as a trifle selfish, people who would rather demand a silent hour on their own than mingle with families and friends. To some kids I taught, it was bunnyhopping around the room imitating lotus posture chanting 'aum'! Most stereotypes are wrong, and I'm inclined to dislike all generalizations on principle. No one is more or less than an individual, or more or less than what they uniquely are. So if you're reading this book with a shy look over your shoulder at someone else on the tube train whom you think may be judging you, have my encouragement to be totally individual and proud of it!

Actually, the underground train is quite a good opportunity to embark on a bit of meditation! I don't recommend going for the rather deeper experience of the chapter that preceded this in such a situation – it might lead to a bit of a shock if there is a sudden announcement or an abrupt halt when you are in that deep state. But you do see people meditating on the London tube, and presumably on other underground systems as well. On a crowded train it's strangely powerful to do the standing exercise we first met in chapter one, even when the train is rocking a bit from side to side. If you try it, have something handy to grab on to, because if the train goes over the points all the trust in your grounded footwork is going to be under pretty severe testing. I don't want to be responsible for you being launched across the carriage! You'll certainly have to use your imagination to feel that the ground is solid underneath, but the loose knees will stand you in wonderful stead (that's a revealing phrase when you think about it!) and surprise you with your resilience. In short, the posture in which you begin meditation is remarkably like a dance posture and similar to the one sailors have to adopt on a moving ship. It's not heavy, except in the weight we first lay down on the earth.

Ah, you'll perhaps say, one thing I won't be able to do on the tube is to feel anything like sunlight filling me when I breathe. Here I can only speak from personal experience, but I'd rather say that the opposite is true: I've had a wonderful sense of 'the light' (by which I mean something beyond the physical) at times when I'm right underground, far from the sun's rays, far from the nearest wi-fi signal, dead to all electronic communication. I can't quite explain this: maybe the subterranean environment is in its own way rather protective, and we thus discover a surprisingly useful form of safety. I can only say that I've known it work, really well, and I've also been tremendously aware that I can radiate light. It feels as though that little enclosed world simply concentrates the power.

Anyway, the point is that you don't have to set aside long hours to meditate. Teachers get us meditating at set times of day only because our body clock then works in partnership with us, and helps us remember to do what we're doing. In terms of tapping consciousness beyond the present one, such as feeling the breath body, I think we need all the practice we can get, practice at the different skills of meditation one after another. Thus ten minutes in a good standing posture on the tube, or twenty minutes sitting out of the worst of the crush on a bus, are not to be sniffed at!

Working around obstacles is good for building concentration, too. If you don't agree, then just ignore this section of the book!

*

Back in chapter one, I promised that I'd talk more about how meditation can bring energy. Here you have it: standing and meditating, as the train rocks this way and that, you are alive and vital. You are not getting tired because you are not fighting life, or boredom, all the time: you are with life every moment of the day – at every stop the train makes – and you are still there as it thunders through the tunnel. Life demands that attention always, and our boredom arises from forgetting life.

I assure you that you will be less tired for working in this way, and staying loose and alert.

*

Once, I was at a meeting at which a Buddhist abbot was expected as guest speaker. Most of us had been in the village hall where the meeting took place for a while before he was due. When he came, I was at the opposite end of the room from the one by which he entered. Looking down the room towards him I had a strange sensation of greater-than-usual space around his body, as he engaged in little conversations and slowly progressed towards the daïs. It was odd, because it wasn't an obvious physical space around him, and in some ways people were pressing him quite close: it just felt that however close they came there was always air, or room, or a sort of dignity around his person.

Then he came forward to speak, and did little more than talk for a few minutes about his spiritual practice and the potential for ours, but in a way that held our attention totally, before he moved on to questions. When someone asked a question about how not to fall asleep in meditation, I was particularly interested as, struggling as I do with slight sleep apnoea, I can sometimes find staying alert a real problem. He made a couple of suggestions, and then reminded us that if it's a real problem for us (and if we don't just need sleep!) a largely failsafe answer is to do a standing meditation.

He stood there demonstrating it, and as he stood I had the strongest sense I have known of sheer presence. *Before us was a human body radiating light.* This was a while ago, and though I had already come to use the standing exercise we began with, I hadn't thought of it being one to sustain meditation, for substantial periods. What the Buddhist abbot taught, though, was almost identical to what I was already doing. Only he went on to describe what happens when we do hold the standing posture for quite a while. One regular pattern, for instance, is that however much thought we put into relaxing the body, from one end to the other, in the standing posture we have an unerring tendency to put tension back into our shoulders, even when we have just let it go. Part of the discipline of a standing meditation, therefore, is to check out our shoulders every minute or two, and be conscious about relaxing them again. And again and again.

Of course, that's one reason we stay awake! It's the shoulders that need checking

most often, but we need to check out any-
where in the body that we know in our own
case is particularly subject to tensing up.* It
may be the solar plexus muscles, or it may
be that we are prone to clenching our teeth.
Or our sacrum and base of spine. Everyone
is individual in where they most often keep
their attention (and where they store their
tension): it's just that in the standing posture
the shoulders are in the front line.

For me, the remarkable thing is the number
of people I have worked with who right from
the start have found it easy to meditate in the
standing posture. They say, as I do, that alertness
comes more readily, that concentration is easier
too – at least up to a point. I can't claim to have
meditated with a standing group for more than
twenty or thirty minutes, so the deep experiences in chapter five won't usually have hap-
pened then. Working with a group, I like to get
each participant to do their standing meditation in front of their chair, which they've al-

*See the list on p. 138

ready prepared with the number of cushions they usually like, and simply allow them to sit down as soon as they think the standing posture is hindering rather than helping their focus.

*

Strictly speaking, sitting in a chair isn't a traditional posture for meditation. Most people know what the lotus posture looks like, with the legs not just crossed but woven over one another till the soles face up. The base of the spine is either touching the ground, or just supported by a seat that rises at the back, or by a wedge of cushion. I haven't done a lot of research, and I generally sit on a chair, but I suspect there is a longer tradition behind a standing meditation than a seated one. In particular, the standing posture resonates with what we know of the Native Americans – although many would not describe a Native American, standing on a bluff or crag with eyes upon the horizon as meditating. If meditation is primarily a technique in which we simply become utterly, and richly, aware of the present (as I would agree it is) then the Native Americans are a wonderful model.

The image of the Native American standing on the bluff is one of someone absolutely
absorbed in the here and now, looking out
across the landscape. It is also an image of
athleticism, of absorption, of alertness. Above
is the broad sky and below the dry earth, so
that although the man (or the woman) is absorbed in the horizontals of the landscape, he
is polarized too between earth and sky.

The ancient Egyptians fascinated Vanda
Scaravelli, with the extraordinarily elongated
standing posture we see in their monuments
and artefacts. She saw them as knowing a se-
cret about the body, which is that the spine is
pivoted at the fifth lumbar vertebra, and that
the lower body sinks down with this, from
gravity, while the upper body lifts. Again, we
have the image of the earth and sky conjoined
in the body, and serving (as the trunk of a tree
serves) to carry energy between the two. The
Egyptian priest kings stood with the right foot
just in front of the left rather than evenly apart,

as we have become used to doing.

The Egyptian posture works in a chair, too, though. If you wish to start your meditation in a place of great strength, begin it by sitting down from the standing posture, keeping as much as possible of what you learnt  in that posture, keeping your back extended and upright, the gaze ahead. Seated, place both feet on the floor, and allow the hands to relax palm upright and out on each knee. I cannot start in this way without feeling an enormous strength, which I link with ancient Egypt. I call it the kingly pose, but it is really just how the pharaohs sat, if you look at the pictures.

After I have felt that strength and used it to

help me find a steady breath, then I cross my right ankle over my left, as my teacher White Eagle advises, and cup my left hand in my right, in my lap. That is a 'sealed-system' posture that is right for the deeper meditation and helps to insulate you against shocks like external noise.

The practised meditator is very self-contained. The moment matters; the next moment does not. Very recently, someone in a class described being stranded seventy miles from home with a ninety-year-old dependent. Although the one she was looking after was in great panic, my student seems to have been completely unfazed by the situation and was totally calm. In this frame of mind she rescued them both, at her own expense. The meditation lifestyle helps you cope in crisis, and it is not particularly worried about small financial details either!

CHAPTER SEVEN

Meditation ... is Health

Meditation goes beyond the causes of illness

THERE are plenty of books about the benefits of meditation. Every year, new benefits are verified by scientific studies. 'If you stay in a contemplative state for twenty minutes', says one of them, 'your experiences will tend to feel more real, affecting your nervous system in ways that enhance physical and emotional health. Antistress hormones and neurochemicals are released throughout the body, as well as pleasure-enhancing and depression-decreasing neurotransmitters like dopamine and serotonin. Even ten to fifteen minutes of meditation appears to have significantly positive effects on cognition, relaxation and psychological health, and it has been shown to reduce smoking and binge-drinking behaviour.'*

The same author reminds us how good things like yawning and smiling are, not just for our general health but good for the brain in particular. It seems that the things that help us are many of them very simple indeed.

Meditation and mindfulness (which is very similar), are frequently sold as stress-busters. A friend of mine teaches 'endorphin meditation', which in layman's terms is just a reminder that meditation tends to make us happy when we do it, and happiness is most certainly an antidote to stress.

There are also lots of books about neuroscience and meditation. Some of them say different things, but it's not unfair to summarize them with the suggestion that one of the things about meditation is that it's a whole-brain activity. It involves even the most primitive part of the brain, the old reptilian brain. We met that when talking of meditation as developing the anterior cingulate, the bit of

*Newberg and Waldman, p. 159

the brain that enables us to control the primal fear/flight response. There is some suggestion that in involving this part of the brain without prompting fear or flight, meditation discovers a simple and unified sense of being that we simply cannot describe because it is properly located in a part of brain that goes back before language. At all events, such general stimulation of the brain seems to be good for it in a way that worry is not!

I'd like to suggest, though, that one of the reasons we support our health through meditation is that we make the moment itself so powerful and rich. (See the sections about living within the moment in chapters two and three.) Within the moment, you are not only safe, you are both well and creative. You are in charge of your life, not toppled by it. That is because by bringing your consciousness into that very safe space, the moment, you are very aware of your strength of being, from the moment you relax into the first breath to the very moment you expel the last of it. You are awake, as the Buddha liked to say; you are highly alive.

The niyamas (the second Limb of yoga) surprise many people by including the word tapas, which is often translated as 'enthusiasm'. Jenny Beeken writes: 'The Sanskrit root ... means 'to blaze'. This is the inner fire that urges us on to develop, to achieve, to love life and all that we do.'* Hopefully, tapas applies to our meditation practice; if through that our approach to the whole of life is enthusiasm, then the whole of life is more spontaneous, more full of creative fire, and effortless in that there is no inner struggle about what we do. It's no surprise that meditation is a cure for stress, but not just because of its reflective elements. It's because in the moment, if it is utterly involving, there is total creativity and zero fear.

While the niyamas in yoga describe qualities within our relationship to ourselves, the first Limb of yoga, the yamas, mainly describe

*Jenny Beeken, YOGA OF THE HEART, second edition. Liss, Hants. (White Eagle Publishing Trust), 2000 , p. 35

qualities that may govern our relationship to others. As well as *ahimsa*, non-violence, they include *satya*, truth, *asteya*, non-stealing, and *aparigraha*, non-possessiveness. There is also *brahmacharya*, reverence for the creative life-force within. This is often translated as celibacy, too, but there's no need to take it in the strict, ascetic sense, so much as remaining in self-awareness rather than losing the self in sense-immersion. Meanwhile *satya*, truth, was actually Gandhi's great rallying call to himself, not *ahimsa* – something people often forget. He meant it with regard to his own self, but also in regard to other people, and it was what propelled his activity in the world, what led his crusades against all sorts of oppression. Oppressing another, he felt, was the most baisc contravention of truth.*

If the *yamas* are seen as key qualities that go along with meditation, then meditation, like truth, is not only about self-relation but about

*The idea of *satyagraha*, search for truth, is beautifully worked out in Philip Glass's opera of that name (1980).

our relations with others. Meditation at its best is not a reclusive activity, but a social one. Even in the Upanishads, written over two thousand years ago, the twin pillars of our self-unfoldment are meditation and service, service to others. The form of meditation taught by my own teacher, White Eagle, is ideally meditation within a group: a social activity, with a strong measure of shared experience, not a uniquely personal one. The key quality his teaching seeks to bring out in us is kindness to one another.

A modern perspective on spirituality is that it is not so much about aspiration as interaction. 'The spirituality of persons is developed and revealed primarily in their relations with other persons', says one author I read recently.* He continues: 'If you regard spirituality as centrally about liberating relations between people, then a new era of participative religion opens up, and this calls for a radical restructuring and reappraisal of tradi-

*John Heron, PARTICIPATORY SPIRITUALITY: A FAREWELL TO AUTHORITARIAN RELIGION. N. Carolina (Lulu Press), 2006, p. 6

tional spiritual maps and rules.'

When I therefore write of meditation as health, it must cover not only physical health but spiritual health too – and that means health in our interpersonal relations. We treat each other mindfully when we practice meditation; we slowly learn to understand one another individually and collectively, because the experience we discover within meditation is actually universal. It crosses boundaries.

*

Our antipathies towards one another all arise, ultimately, out of fear. In fear we look upon each other as a threat – even people whom we love – the moment we perceive that they might take something from us. One of the reasons meditation is able to help in this respect is that it builds up values that are located in the moment, not moments yet to come. Technically, we cannot lose anything in the truly meditative life, because loss is a comparison between one moment and another, whereas meditation only recognizes the moment that is happening, now. This is the principle behind a rather misunderstood Buddhist concept, non-attachment. Some people seem almost to punish themselves with this idea, as though it involves active rejection of any hold things seem to have over them. When you live entirely in the sufficiency of the moment, nothing is attached anyway. And when you are attached to nothing, the fear of loss is meaningless.

Living in the moment does not mean that every moment is spent in introspection, trying to get it right. It's just a habit of mind, a constant asking of yourself, 'Where am I in all of this?' If you ask the question aright, the sense of poise that comes enables you to be present to external things simultaneously with your self-awareness.

In common with many other people, one of the things I love about living in England is the passage of the seasons. It's not just the ever-changing weather pattern and the amount of sunlight, but the things in nature that are only available at a certain season. Thus, in the spring season I am often out hunting around for wild garlic, which is delicious in cooking and in salads and is only available for a month or two. To find and pick the wild garlic is a little ritual for me (just as meditation is) and while I am collecting it I am absorbed in the uniqueness of its long green leaves, its beautiful white flowers and (above all) the smell that rises from the banks of garlic, which is cleansing and strangely intoxicating at the same time. I am quite wrapped up in what I am doing. You might argue that the experience is not transcendent, but it is intensely mindful.

*

Transcendence is a word I haven't used about meditation, yet. That's because I am so keen, both in my own meditations and when I teach meditation, to work from a really grounded place – hence the standing start that I described at the beginning of this book. I've also pointed out that it is precisely when we are most aware of our feet (our 'understandings', my aunt loved to call them) that we are also most ready to lift our consciousness above the everyday. Connected to the earth, we are safe to experience our breath body. I've tried to show that awareness of the breath body in meditation is only the beginning.

Prepare in your usual way for meditation, but feel the heels' contact with the ground, or in a seated position feel the earth through the base of your spine. Remember how I remarked that we can be alive on what people call the etheric plane simply by being in contact with the earth and being happy. Difficult though happiness may be to find when you are feeling sad or worried, the very safety that the ground offers can be the first stage in going beyond those emotions. The next is to breathe yourself into the moment, and feel its richness.

As you are breathing, in this aware way, relax your face muscles, even if you have already done so once. With practice, relaxing your facial muscles can lead to what is known as the 'inner smile' or the 'Buddha smile'. It is not necessarily visible externally as a smile (the quality we most associate with the Buddha's smile is traditionally compassion, not happiness) but it does have to do with a contentment, an absorption in whatever the present moment offers. And the present moment needn't offer you worry, because the present is the present and worries are by definition related to the future. *That future may simply never happen.* I mean that not as a cheering-up message, but as a statement about the present; the future is beyond consideration. The sanctity of the present moment offers not a single clue as to what the next moment will offer. And if the seeming worst ever does happen, you are still absolutely safe in that next moment too, although it may seem impossibly hard (until you have practised it, constantly) to get away from fears about the moments that succeed one another.

Conscious of your smile more than anything in the world, your inner smile, explore not just the length of the moment but its breadth.... Feel how infinitely rich it is, how full of light, just like your smile. Safe on the earth, you are also rising in consciousness, looking down now on the physical form that is cross-legged, or seated, or standing, beneath you. A sense of the air around you makes the breath very real. This is your breath body, and you can live in it, quite happily, during this moment. But your rising seems almost to continue, the world of your awareness getting ever larger. The universe is infinite, and you are no less infinite than the whole universe. The Big Bang is an event that is happening, continuing, now – and you are part of it.

There is no you and it, only oneness. Explore this consciousness, moment by moment. Every breath is a new birth into cosmic awareness. Linear time is something you can look at as an illusion, remote from you. Presence in the oneness comes from an awareness that you are nothing but light.

Your light could create or heal anything on the limited earth. If there is any geography to be found in your consciousness now, it contains a sense that you are on a plane way above the earth. Look down into the problems you face on the earth, not so much identifying them — you do not want to resurrect them in your consciousness — as shedding light onto them.

It is as though they are in a cave, and if you saw it with your earthly vision the cave would seem to be all darkness. Right now, you are light, and when you shine your light into the cave, you may realize that the very things that troubled you are all jewels. The jewels of your life-experience, transformed.

*

An experience that is so deep as this demands that as you bring yourself back to everyday consciousness, which at some time you must, you do so very much in control of yourself. You have been experiencing light; now breathe it into your very body, every cell of your physical body. Let the body awaken in the awareness of its cells being light. When every cell of your body is alive with light, you are really creating health by your visualization.

Using the lungs like this, though, will also make you much more aware of your physical body than you were. Go with this until you are not just aware of the movement of your lungs, but of your feet on the ground, of the air in the room, of any part of the body that perhaps has stiffened and needs to be stretched – and let your stretching really 'bring you back to earth'. This breathing yourself back into the body is good to do at the end of any meditation, and particularly if you are inclined to feel hypersensitive afterwards, which some people are.

There is an ancient yoga practice of breathing a circle of light around us after meditation. You breathe out, and then on the inbreath you imagine a line of light which comes up from under the left foot, round the lefthand side of the body, breathing in all the time. By the time you are full of breath, you have half-encircled the body, as far as the crown of the head. On the outbreath, you bring the line of light down the righthand side and complete it under the right foot. This leads you into another breath, and another, right up to seven.

Next, having really emptied your lungs, you imagine this same line of light going around you clockwise (as you look down on it) slowly rising in a spiral so that by the time there are seven rings to the spiral your lungs are full and the line of light is over your head. Now release the breath and imagine the light coming right down through your body, right through the central nervous system and the spine, until it goes down into the earth, so that you are balanced by the first part of the exercise and grounded by the second.

In yoga anatomy, you are working with channels of energy in the body known as *nadis*. They link with the energy centres known as *chakras*. If you know where those are, you would have preceded the breathing part of the exercise by imagining each one of these 'sealed'. Your seal could consist of an equal-sided cross composed only of light and surrounded by a circle of light ... drawn onto the crown, the brow, the throat, the heart, the solar plexus, the sacral centre and the base of the spine.

Sip a glass of water to bring yourself right back.

*

Although meditation fits well with a vocabulary borrowed from India, the symbols of transcendence are deeply present in Christianity. If we see the life of Jesus as symbolic, then the ascent of the mountain that precedes the transfiguration, for instance, is a perfect metaphor for transcendence in meditation. The Sermon on the Mount was just that; and to be ready for their Master, the disciples gathered 'with one accord' in an 'upper room'.

CHAPTER EIGHT

Meditation ... is Completeness

Meditating is about both living and dying

ONE THING about living in the moment is that because you truly attend to it, every moment is consciously begun and completed. You welcome the new breath, you watch it to fullness the same way a wave lifts to fullness, and continue as the wave collapses, runs up the beach, and ceases before the next forms. You are born with the breath and you die with the breath – except that there is something in the body which until the very last moment of your life leads you spontaneously forward into the next moment, the next breath.

Yet even though taking a breath is involuntary (a relaxation, as I said above), we are making it voluntary by being conscious of it and welcoming it. No, we are not going to stop breathing just because we feel like it, even if sometimes life feels so hard we'd quite like to. Meditation is a greater engagement with life and with the moment than one that would allow us to give up as easily as that. Yet it is said that the experienced yogi or yogina in India counts his or her breaths and – at last recognizing the moment has come – simply does not take the next breath. The Native American is said to have been able to develop a conscious openness to death, not dissimilar from that. Before my own mother died, I had a strong sense that she knew very clearly that the moment was coming when, rather than renewing her connection with the physical plane with the breath she took, she would breathe only light, not oxygen, and take her way through the portals of light.

We don't often talk about death in this way, but this book has been about an experience of meditation completely related to each moment as though nothing but that moment mattered. It is therefore completely reasonable

to see death as a part, not an end, of the meditation experience, the meditation lifestyle.
Christian mystics have often talked of life only
as a preparation for death, and advocated a
spiritual practice in which we consciously 'die
to the world' over and over. Where their dying to the world was perhaps a kind of asceti-
cism, meditational dying to the world is not
caught up with the process of rejection, but
with openness to the All.

When you are safe in the moment, through
meditation, nothing matters except the moment. Moreover, you are used to dying, because every breath is completed with a death
and a rebirth, as each one gives way to the next.

*

To talk about completeness has also to do with
our practice being a complete one. We get
used to a defined period of meditation in the
morning or in the evening but then we are,
perhaps, only at the beginning of practice. This
book has sought to offer ways in which this
occasional practice (I don't necessarily mean

infrequent, for the morning and evening session may be done with faithful regularity) might be transformed into one that carries a meditational consciousness into all areas of life and all times of day.

Regular morning or evening meditations create a kind of ritual. We do the practice maybe the same way every time: retiring to a particular room, a particular chair, facing a particular window or picture. Each time, we put a rose, or another flower, or a gentle flame in front of us to help us focus our practice. And so on. The repetition builds a message into our body that prepares us for the moment of meditation.

But the day has a great many more rituals: our trip to work, our cleaning of the house – or just of our teeth – our preparation of food and our saying goodnight to the children, or our partner. As I've already shown with my story about harvesting wild garlic, we can bring a form of meditation into all of these little rituals. We just make them conscious, and enjoy them consciously, moment by moment. Regarding them in this way, you can both know what you are doing and love doing it. Love even your foibles! Thus you convert the way you experience even boring things into something that leads you in the direction of meditation.

It's become almost commonplace to say that waiting at a red light in the car is an opportunity for instant meditation. So is every moment you are kept waiting – and slowly the activity you experience in these moments will become more and more the norm in life, not the exception. Meditation is for all the time.

*

Another way to make meditation into a complete experience, not an occasional one, is to become very experienced in the practice, described earlier in this book (pp. 44, 93), of radiating light into the world. This means being very conscious not just of having light within us but actually being light. That's something we can develop in our everyday practice, and slowly bring out into a consciousness that infuses every moment. Practice grows into practice, and before long we are anticipating and overcoming moments of difficulty by remaining in this awareness of light. The shining six-pointed star was the specific vehicle of light that we considered. White Eagle says: 'Darkness cannot touch you if you are radiating light'.*

In this respect, the spectacle of other people's suffering, and the knowledge of generalized suffering around the globe, is actually part of our liberation. Suffering (including our own, if we regard it carefully) brings out the human sympathies. We hate the spectacle of another grieving or fearing, and so move into compassionate mode. Maybe we succeed in helping, and have the joy of hearing that we have helped. It does not matter, however, whether we get the praise or thanks or not, because the very fact that we have been drawn into our sympathies has led us to think compassionately of those who are suffering. Compassion is an awareness with which the mo-

*THE BOOK OF STAR LIGHT. Liss (W.E.P.T.), 1999, p. 37

ment can be filled, a conscious choice.

Draw the compassion into as many moments of your life as you possibly can, whenever you remember, and you are progressively
moving towards being 'light-filled' – that is,
one who, like the Buddhist abbot I mentioned,
positively radiates light. I don't suppose he
has any more sense that he is visibly radiating
light than you or I do, but our practice leads
us into such a rich place as this.

*

Regular meditation will also help us, as I believe it did my mother, to cross the threshold
into another life seamlessly and without pain
arising from the transition itself. Her own
book about meditation was called A WAY TO HAP-
PINESS, and she chose the title very carefully. She
would say: 'Just try to let the experience you
encounter in meditation, the sense you have of
peace and intense beauty, become ever more
real to you and more constant as life unfolds'.

CHAPTER NINE

Meditation ... is Easy

Every meditator is a beginner

ONE OF the reasons this book is in the order it is, with the chapter most to do with how to meditate coming last, is the concept of 'beginner mind'. Every time you meditate, according to Buddhism, you approach it as though it is something you have never done before. I've said several times now that every breath you take is a completely new experience, in no way tied in quality to the last. Thus everything in this book can be used by a meditator at any level, and anything in this book is something that any meditator can come back to.

It's possible, though, that you have read it through and are still not quite sure what you need to do in order to be sure that your experience 'counts' as meditation, because you are relatively new to the practice – the more so because in quite a major way this book is dedicated to showing that meditation arises out of some of the simplest things we do in life. It also takes you into some quite deep practices – which may be there from the beginning or which may come with time, maybe a long time. To go easily into meditation, the first thing my own teacher (White Eagle) advises is 'to listen'. To people and to nature alike. That is, whenever you can don't let only the eyes work – listen hard for sounds that take your attention to the present, even with human communication. Experience the present deeply, and the rest will follow – it's as simple as that.

The next thing I would ask those who are not sure whether they are really meditating is: 'Why should there be a dividing line between what is meditation and what is not quite?' For me, the defining experience of what meditation might offer is a not infrequent one when I'm in nature. It's the moment when you walk along, maybe wrapped in thoughts and even troubles, and suddenly notice that the birds are singing. Your heart leaps, the moment is beautiful, and what is happening in the present quite pushes out of the way the thoughts you were having, which almost inevitably will have been about the future or the past, or miles away from the here and now. All of a sudden you are very 'here and now' indeed – and normally birdsong has a joyful effect on us.

Practising meditation somehow implies that you are actually looking for an experience like this, maybe a profounder one still. The problem is that if you really want this sort of 'birdsong experience' you'll almost certainly not be able to get round your 'wanting it' nature in order to have the experience. Wanting it will be your experience, while having it is different.

So what the training meditation demands is not so much about what you do, as what you strip away. That's fears, expectations and memories, principally – anything that preoccupies you and stops you 'hearing the birds'. Okay,

it's not all stripping things away: you'll probably establish a little ritual of having a favourite
chair, a favourite place to put it, and a favourite object of concentration in front of you. But

you don't have to – your walk in nature may
be what takes you deeply into meditation first.

I've put some separate notes on posture,
breathing and relaxation in an appendix so that
they can become habitual parts of your preparation. Yet as you begin your meditation, you
don't really want to be thinking: 'What did I do
last time?' or 'How can I imitate that beautiful

experience so-and-so had?', and you certainly don't want to be thinking, 'What's the latest news from the Middle East?' All those thoughts take you away from the present, not into it.

You'd be better, once your little ritual of preparing your space has got you into the right frame of mind, to begin by looking around you and noticing what's there. It doesn't matter if it is the same as it was yesterday or not, this is a different moment and the comparison won't help. Mindfulness of the room you are in both grounds you and opens the doors of perception. Just take in what's around you for what it is – now. Don't get caught up in whether you like everything or not, just notice that it's there. Use your ears as much as your eyes (your brain can sometimes even know the size of a room from tiny echoes) and the other senses even more, if there is anything to smell, taste or touch. Taste is of course a bit unlikely and touch – unless you want to go round the room before you sit down – will be more a question of imagining what things would be like to the touch than actually touching. Be aware of everything but avoid giving special importance to anything. In the main, sounds draw you into the present whereas what the eye sees can take you out of it.

Once you feel very aware of your environment, sounds and all (even that nearby airport or the busy road under the window), start to turn your attention to one thing, normally the object of focus you put out in front of you. I'll assume it's either a flame or a flower, or a picture of the Buddha, or Jesus, or the Dalai Lama, or even that old wrinkled face I spoke of in chapter five, with the light in her eyes. Or it may be a lotus of your imagination. Whatever it is, this is now your focus of attention; try to be absolutely intent upon it, so that nothing else intrudes.

Don't worry if something does intrude, because it will, sooner or later, and you have got to get used to that.

At some point you are going to turn from the point of focus to be again really present, and to remember in a general way the whole roomful of objects that you saw and heard first. Only now you are going to see everything as lovely, as somehow part of a space within yourself which is lovely. I do mean 'lovely' – something worthy of your loving it. Think back to the object of concentration, inwardly, not opening your eyes, and bring the whole picture together. Don't cut yourself off from your feelings – they are very active at this point, but very simple.

*

Many times you will just stay with what is there, perhaps in a slightly value-added kind of a way. If you have chosen really to focus on beauty, that will tend to stimulate your heart without worrying your mind. Moments will start to come, though, when faced with both focusing on one thing and (following the instructions) not focusing on any one thing more than another will push your mind out of the way. Concentration will become an activity in itself, and you won't discriminate between any of the objects you might be focusing on. You won't even be conscious of yourself looking at or listening to them. There will be just a sense of being, of total objectless concentration – of one life only that is neither just personal nor just universal.

There are many ways you can help yourself into this state. The White Eagle quotation I gave on pp. 75ff spoke of it as sometimes feeling like a blankness, 'an emptiness even'. If so, your response must be to trust that blankness if you are going to go through the transformation he describes. In meditation, if you began by using your mind to visualize, there will normally have to be a moment when you recognize your concentration coming from your heart rather than your head – in short, the trust needed for emptiness to become all-ness is akin to allowing awareness to drop trustingly from the head into the heart. That's why it links with the images of beauty I've described.

My sister-in-law Anna puts it a different way, and a variety of ways to understand it and go there can only help. She would tell you to lose yourself in an appreciation of beauty, maybe initially seen externally but later internally. She might say that the moment I describe is the one when you cease to be directing your imagination, but the inner imagination almost takes over; the things you see are somehow spontaneous, not things you create. That does not mean they will be 'odd', so much as that you will go from beauty into beauty. There will be a loss of self-awareness, and instead an absorption in what is all-penetrating or even universal. She speaks of your 'etheric vision' being in control.

Whatever happens, and whether the experience is primarily visual or seems to employ other senses, 'going from beauty into beauty' will tend to be part of the experience. You want at this moment in your meditation really to aspire to the 'highest', 'most light-filled', 'most holy' thing you can imagine, for that is the way you will get the purest communion with all life.

And that is what you want, whatever your technique: to simulate — no, *actually experience* — the moment when the one thing becomes again part of the whole. You can do that at quite a simple level, and enjoy the experience, or it can be the most profound experience of your life, maybe unsought. 'The dewdrop slips into the shining sea' is the classic image given for it.

If you are not pressed for time, it does not matter (within reason) how long you hold the peak experience. Don't feel you have to rush back from it, if you can afford to stay. In terms of 'rising' through the breath body and bodies above that, you may have gone right through to a brief reunion with universal being, a moment of yoga, or union. You will have to descend from this very high place, and the general wisdom is to do it gently. Imagine yourself coming down through levels of beauty, one after another, or descending the mountainside. Come into gentle green valleys where you can be at peace, and recover the very solid physical body that you had at the beginning, or its light-filled replica.

If you did not feel you 'got there', the concept of beginner mind (see the start of this chapter) will help you repeat all of the process, perhaps more successfully, tomorrow. Never ever be discouraged, even if you fall asleep every time you try for month after month (you won't be the first!). All the partial experiences will one day accumulate into one big one, and get you over what may be the biggest but also final hurdle. Finish with the sealing routine at the end of chapter seven (pp. 112–5), set out in note form in the Appendix (pp. 140–2), to balance yourself before you face the world. If you end in a good place, you will start in a good place next time – just like trainers say in the gym as you 'cool down' at the end. In both activities, 'cooling down' is just as important as 'warming up'. And the sealing routine described is part of your cooling down.

Enjoy your meditation – this book is dedicated to allowing you to do that.

Epilogue (... is Forever)

IT'S JUST June, and I'm in Wales, loosening up muscles after six or seven somewhat over-strenuous hours on the hills a day ago. We've walked up a magical little valley in sunshine, yellow flag irises spreading out across the flood plain of the stream on our right, and mysteriously-angled rock formations sporting extensive green moss, ferns of several kinds, and trees growing out of the rock itself. Right now I'm on top of a rocky mound, out of the valley itself and with a rising ridge extending up from it to a strikingly conical mountain, and a view of many others – with Snowdon, just in cloud, at their centre.

It seems a moment to meditate. Not to meditate in any formal way, but just to sit down on an obvious rock seat on the mound. A small oak tree is growing out of the rock ahead; an elder is in flower, and there are foxgloves, and a creeping white flower whose name I have forgotten coming through the sparse turf. Initially, meditation seems scarcely necessary – for this earth is so beautiful – but I am familiar with the knowledge that the better we are are attuned to the physical world, the better our awareness of the inner or 'higher' realms grows. And so I am allowing myself to lighten, slip the bonds, and the landscape beyond my closed eyes at once feels free, and airy. I get a flash of something which feels very Welsh – a flame, a sword, or maybe the post of a Welsh harp, but silvery gold – and know that I could stay in what feels to be an enhanced magical world beyond this one. But I seek something higher, and to relax further is to open myself to a vision which seems to be of what created this beauty – an unknown power, illimitable and loving. This awareness is beyond form, but not beyond feeling. As I rise further, my vision feels absolutely without bounds. I feel both loved, and part of the creative principle itself.

Beauty is as great as we know how to cre-

– 134 –

ate it and allow it. It is the belief of this book first that we can be meditating in an instant if we allow ourselves a connection with nature and its beauty, and that the more we practise the easier this becomes. With careful training of consciousness, we can be meditating silently even when there is an outward concentration on something else. Secondly, my belief is that by meditating we actually fill the world with light at the same time as we fill ourselves. The more we are ourselves light-filled, the greater the beauty we can envision and the more beautiful a world we actually create. And the more that we allow the light to enter our own dark corners, fill them with light as if the light were shining into darkness, and the darkness not comprehending it, the more the darknesses of the world will be transformed, one by one, into light.

Appendices

Appendix A: **Relaxation**

It's rather humbling, given the amount of time we give to relaxation before meditation in the West, that all the first five Limbs of yoga are to calm the body before the three final Limbs (which are all the meditation stages) are explored. What to do to relax the body instead, if you are not proficient in yoga, is outside the compass of this book but well within what you might ask a yoga teacher. Ideally, we would do a set of loosening-up exercises before ever we took our place in the meditation room. In the meditation itself, my suggestion would be to concentrate on relaxing the parts of the body actually most likely to contain or hold tension.

As I go through my own personal checklist, there is a moment when each part of me in turn seems to light up and prepare itself for attention. As I go into meditation, I like to watch:

The brow
The cheek muscles
The jaw and tongue
The neck
The shoulders
The hands
The muscles around the solar plexus
The abdomen and base of the spine

To think back into the facial muscles afterwards is a good way of sustaining and co-ordinating your relaxation, while the exercise (p. 28n) where you let the spine lengthen out is also helpful, and possible to do at the thought level even when you are seated.

Appendix B: **Posture**

With its focus on the standing posture most of all, a lot of this book is about posture and so I will only repeat some key points here. First, don't ever let your desire for good posture lead you back into tension the moment you just relaxed! If you follow the instructions in the book, your upper body will lift and your lower body and most of the skeletal system will go with gravity. To go straight from the standing posture to a seated one (particularly if your choice is to use a chair) is a good way to maintain good posture. Just check, both in standing and in sitting, that your shoulders don't rise.

Use the back of the chair if you have to, but try to use it as little as possible, maybe with the idea that one day you will manage without. An upright spine is as much about balance as anything to do with muscles – a good way to achieve it through balance is to do a little rocking back and forth before you find where equilibrium lies. Then you will be like one of those tall piles of stones people love to build on the beach: surprisingly stable, and yet with no external support.

A gently wedge-shaped cushion, lower in front than behind, is a good aid to posture in that it very slightly tilts the pelvis forward and assists the spine in finding balance.

Appendix C: **Breathing**

As I've said in the text, a key point about breathing is not to 'try' but simply to 'observe'. Don't be the slightest bit worried that the moment you look at how you are breathing it all feels artificial and tense, or that you yawn, or never seem to have enough air inside you. Just keep watching, and even if it takes a few minutes, you will eventually be watching the rhythm return. The breath lengthens naturally when you are at peace with it, and your watching will be enough to stop it becoming shallow and incomplete. Above all, watch the outbreath: that's the way you make sure that the inbreath that follows has plenty of room.

Beyond any instruction here, your best way forward, if you want to do more work on the breath, is Jenny Beeken's DON'T HOLD YOUR BREATH.

Appendix D: A **Sealing Routine**

I have put this suggestion in the text already, in chapter six, along with a way of 'coming

down' from meditation by breathing yourself back into the physical body. You can also
use the 'coming down the mountain' way of
visualizing your return to the everyday world,
given at the end of chapter nine.

After you are 'down', use this routine; it's
the one recommended in the White Eagle
School of Meditation. The second and third
parts of it, at least, go back to the *Hatha Yoga
Pradipika*, the great yoga text of the fifteenth
century. There are three stages.

First, mentally draw an equal-sided cross
of light with a circle of light around it (cf p.
114) on the following seven centres or *chakras*.

The crown

The brow

The throat

The heart

The solar plexus

The sacral centre

The base of the spine

Second – you are still drawing with light
– imagine yourself surrounded in light as you

take seven full breaths. This is done by empty-ing the lungs, and then imagining the light coming up the lefthand side of the body (in a semicircle, if you like, or close in if you pre-fer) as you breathe in. By the time this arc has come up over your head, your lungs are full. You then release the breath as you complete the circle, back down to the feet. Do this six more times.

Lastly, still working with a line of light that begins under the feet, from very empty lungs imagine the line spiralling around you clock-wise, rising, so that by the time there are seven rings to the spiral the line is again over your head. Now you draw that line down through the body, down the spine and right down into the ground beneath you.

We use the term 'sealing'; this is also, how-ever, a balancing exercise and the feeling at the end of it is of poise and substantial inner strength.

Index